DIABETIC-FRIENDLY CHRISTMAS COOKIES RECIPES COOKBOOK

TASTY AND EASY TO MAKE SUGAR-FREE DELIGHTS FOR HOLIDAY SEASONS

OLIVIA A. JAMES

Copyright © 2023 by OLIVIA A. JAMES

TABLE OF CONTENT

INTRODUCTION

Amidst the twinkling lights and joyous celebration, there is a silent battle that many people experience over the holidays. The narrative revolves around a yearning for something sugary, the comforting flavour of Christmas cookies, and the struggle one has with one's own health issues, particularly for those managing a tight balance with diabetes.

This narrative has been a part of my life, so I know it well. I'm familiar with the diabetic management routines, so I've experienced the tug between the need for typical holiday goodies and the prudence that comes with limiting sugar intake. The craving for warm cookies without any accompanying anxiety is something I can still clearly recall.

While I was growing up, the kitchen was the heart of my family holiday traditions. It was a place where we gathered, sharing laughter, memories, with the aroma of freshly baked cookies and other delicacies filling the atmosphere. However, the excitement of baking for the holidays started to wane as time passed and the realities of managing diabetes came in.

There was a gap, a want to experience that feeling of togetherness and delight in small pleasures without sacrificing well-being.

DIABETIC-FRIENDLY CHRISTMAS COOKIES RECIPES COOKBOOK is more than just a cookbook. It is a solution to that desire or cravings while still striking a balance in health. It supports the idea that enjoying the pleasures of holiday indulgence shouldn't have to be sacrificed in order to manage diabetes. With empathy and personal experience as my guides, I began a project to develop a compilation of dishes that capture the essence of the holidays without increasing blood sugar.

This book's goal is straightforward but significant. It's about providing a beautiful answer, a link between custom and choices that are health-conscious. It is for anyone who is worried about diabetes, whether they are just diagnosed and looking for blameless ways to celebrate, or they are experienced with managing chronic diabetes for themselves or a loved one and are looking for tasty new recipes.

It aims at transforming Christmas baking by combining happiness and health in one dish. It involves making cookies that aren't just sugar-free, but tastes great and brings back memories. Every dish is a promise of life's celebration, a method to experience the festive spirit without sacrificing any quality, and more than just a set of directions.

It is an invitation to enjoy a festive season full of tasty, diabetic-friendly delights, to rediscover the joy of holiday baking, and to enjoy traditional flavors without the guilt. So come along with me as we reinvent holiday gatherings with the DIABETIC-FRIENDLY CHRISTMAS COOKIES RECIPES COOKBOOK.

EXTRA NOTE

The measurements provided in the recipes are typically meant to yield a certain number of cookies rather than servings for people. The exact number of cookies produced can vary based on the size and shape of the cookies formed from the dough.

However, the quantities listed in the ingredients are generally tailored to produce a batch of cookies sufficient for a small group or family to enjoy during the holiday season or as treats for gatherings. Adjustments can be made to the quantities depending on the number of cookies desired or the number of people expected to enjoy them.

If you have a specific number of servings or cookies needed for an event or gathering, you can scale the recipe accordingly by adjusting the ingredient quantities while maintaining the ratios for best results.

Estimated preparation and baking times for each recipe are approximate and may vary depending on various factors such as individual cooking experience and pace, equipment used, oven efficiency, and specific recipe variations. Adjustments can be made based on personal experience and desired outcomes.

NATURAL AND HEALTHY SUGAR ALTERNATIVES

Here is a list of some sugar alternatives that can be used in place of refined sugar in your recipes. Experiment with these options to find the best fit for your desired taste and dietary needs.

COCONUT SUGAR:

Derived from the sap of coconut palm trees, coconut sugar contains small amounts of nutrients and has a lower glycemic index compared to regular sugar.

DATE PASTE:

Made by blending dates with water, date paste is a natural sweetener rich in fiber and nutrients. It can be used to sweeten recipes.

MAPLE SYRUP:

A natural sweetener extracted from the sap of maple trees, maple syrup contains antioxidants and minerals. Opt for pure maple syrup without added sugars.

HONEY:

A natural sweetener produced by bees, honey contains antioxidants and has potential health benefits. Choose raw and unprocessed varieties for more nutrients.

MOLASSES:

A byproduct of the sugar refining process, molasses contains vitamins and minerals. It has a strong flavor and can be used as a sweetener in certain recipes.

FRUIT PUREES:

Pureed fruits like applesauce, mashed bananas, or pureed berries can add natural sweetness and moisture to baked goods. These natural sweeteners can be used as alternatives to refined sugar in your recipes, providing varying flavors, sweetness levels, and potential health benefits.

STEVIA:

Derived from the leaves of the Stevia rebaudiana plant, stevia is a zero-calorie sweetener that can be used in powder or liquid form.

MONK FRUIT SWEETENER:

Made from monk fruit extract, this sweetener is natural, zero-calorie, and does not spike blood sugar levels.

ERYTHRITOL:

A sugar alcohol with very few calories and a low glycemic index, often used as a sugar substitute in baking due to its similar taste and texture.

XYLITOL:

Another sugar alcohol with a sweetness similar to sugar, often used in baking. It has fewer calories and a lower glycemic index than sugar.

20

EASY-TO-MAKE, MOUTH WATERING AND TASTY SUGAR-FREE CHRISTMAS COOKIES RECIPES.

RECIPE 1: ALMOND FLOUR SNOWBALL COOKIES

These chewy, soft snowball cookies are created with almond flour, shredded coconut, powdered sugar replacement, almond essence, and a dash of salt. Enjoy the traditional Christmas flavors.

Estimated Yield: *20-24 cookies*
Preparation Time: *15-20 minutes*
Baking Time: *12-15 minutes*

INGREDIENTS

½ cup unsweetened shredded coconut

½ cup almond flour

½ cup powdered sugar alternative

A pinch of salt and

½ teaspoon of almond essence

METHOD OF PREPARATION

1. Set oven temperature to 325°F (165°C).

2. Almond flour, shredded coconut, powdered sugar substitute, almond essence, and salt should all be combined in a big basin.

3. Mix thoroughly to create a dough.

4. Form the dough into little balls with a diameter of about one inch.

5. Roll the dough balls and place them on an ungreased baking sheet.

6. Bake for 12 to 15 minutes, or until the cookies start to turn a light golden brown around the edges.

7. After taking the cookies out of the oven, allow them to cool for a few minutes on the baking sheet before moving them to a wire rack to finish cooling.

SERVING SUGGESTIONS

These sugar-free snowball cookies are a great treat for Christmas parties or to have with a cup of tea.

PRESERVATION TIPS

To keep the cookies fresher for longer, freeze them or store them in an airtight jar at room temperature for up to a week.

EXTRA TIP(S)

Roll the cooled cookies in more powdered sugar substitute for a more festive look.

Try varying the flavor by incorporating extracts like vanilla or peppermint into the dough.

RECIPE 2: ALMOND BUTTER COOKIES WITH CINNAMON

These delicious cookies with almond butter and cinnamon will warm your palate with their well-balanced spiciness and nutty flavor.

Estimated Yield: *16-20 cookies*
Preparation Time: *15-20 minutes*
Baking time: *15-18 minutes*

INGREDIENTS

1 cup of almond butter

1 teaspoon finely ground cinnamon

⅓ cup almond flour

⅓ cup sugar alternative

½ teaspoon of baking powder

A dash of salt

METHOD OF PREPARATION:

1. Set oven temperature to 350°F (175°C).

2. Almond butter, cinnamon, almond flour, sugar substitute, baking powder, and salt should all be combined in a big basin and beaten into a dough.

3. Use a fork to gently flatten the balls of dough that you roll into tablespoon-sized pieces.

4. Place the cookies on a baking sheet that has not been oiled.

5. Bake for 10 to 12 minutes, until the edges are browned.

6. After taking the cookies out of the oven, allow them to cool for a few minutes on the baking sheet before moving them to a wire rack to finish cooling.

SERVING SUGGESTIONS

Enjoy these cinnamon almond butter cookies as a healthful treat or as a comfortable snack with a glass of almond milk.

PRESERVATION TIPS

To prolong their shelf life, freeze the cookies or keep them in an airtight container at room temperature for around a week.

EXTRA TIP(S)

Use dark roast almond butter for a deeper flavour.

Give the cookies a dusting of cinnamon sugar before baking for an extra flavour.

RECIPE 3: GINGER-BREAD COOKIES WITHOUT SUGAR

These traditional sugar-free gingerbread cookies, scented with Christmas spices and toasty spices, will help you embrace the festive mood.

Estimated Yield: *16-20 cookies*
Preparation Time: *20-25 minutes*
Baking Time: *10-12 minutes*

INGREDIENTS

1 tablespoon of ground ginger

2 cups of almond flour

1 teaspoons finely ground cinnamon

1/4 tsp finely ground nutmeg

1/4 tsp ground cloves

⅓ cup sugar alternative

2 teaspoons (in moderation) of molasses

½ teaspoon of baking soda

A dash of salt

METHOD OF PREPARATION

1. Set oven temperature to 350°F (175°C).

2. Mix almond flour, sugar replacement, molasses, baking soda, salt, and spices in a big basin until a dough forms.

3. To firm up, chill the dough in the refrigerator for fifteen to twenty minutes.

4. On a surface dusted with flour, roll out the dough to a thickness of about ¼ inch.

5. Cut out the shapes you want using cookie cutters.

6. Put the cut-out cookies onto a baking sheet that hasn't been oiled.

7. Bake for 10 to 12 minutes, or until the edges start to crisp up.

8. After taking the cookies out of the oven, allow them to cool for a few minutes on the baking sheet before moving them to a wire rack to finish cooling.

SERVING

With these sugar-free versions, you can still Enjoy the festive flavor of ginger-bread without feeling guilty. Use sprinkles or frosting to adorn the cookies to add even more festive flair.

PRESERVATION TIPS

To extend the cookies' shelf life, freeze them or keep them in an airtight container at room temperature.

EXTRA TIP(S)

Increase the amount of ground ginger in the dough by one teaspoon for a stronger gingerbread flavor.

Utilizing various forms of cookie cutters, craft festive forms such as gingerbread men, snowflakes and Christmas trees.

RECIPE 4: MACAROONS MADE WITH COCONUT

Enjoy these classic coconut macaroons, which are created with shredded coconut, egg whites, sugar substitute, and a touch of vanilla essence. They are light and fluffy.

Estimated Yield: 16-20 cookies
Preparation Time: 15-20 minutes
Baking time: 15-18 minutes

INGREDIENTS

3 cups of shredded unsweetened coconut

4 beaten egg whites

⅓ cup sugar alternative

1 teaspoon vanilla extract, one pinch salt

METHOD OF PREPARATION

1.   Set oven temperature to 175°C/350°F.

2. Shredded coconut, egg whites, sugar replacement, vanilla essence, and salt should all be thoroughly mixed together in a big bowl.

3. Drop mixture onto ungreased baking sheets in rounded teaspoons.

4. The macaroons should be baked for 20 to 25 minutes, or until they are golden brown and just firm to the touch.

5. After taking the macaroons out of the oven, let them cool fully on the baking sheets.

SERVING SUGGESTION

Enjoy these airy and fluffy coconut macaroons as a blameless afternoon snack or dessert. They are a great delicacy for any occasion because of their delicate texture and gentle sweetness.

PRESERVATION TIPS

To extend the shelf life of the macaroons, freeze them or keep them in an airtight container at room temperature for up to a week.

EXTRA TIP(S)

Use toasted shredded coconut for a deeper taste.

For a rich treat, dunk the macaroons in melted chocolate.

RECIPE 5: NON-SUGAR COATED OATMEAL RAISIN COOKIES

Enjoy the healthful taste of these oatmeal raisin cookies, which are made with rolled oats, almond flour, raisins, sugar replacement, eggs, vanilla essence, and cinnamon. They're a healthier take on a beloved dessert.

Estimated Yield: *18-22 cookies*

Preparation Time: *20-25 minutes*

Baking time: *10-12 minutes*

INGREDIENTS

1 cup almond flour

2 cups rolled oats

1/4 cup of raisins

⅓ cup sugar alternative

2 Eggs

1/2 teaspoon of vanilla essence

½ teaspoon of cinnamon

METHOD OF PREPARATION

1. Set oven temperature to 175°C/350°F.
2. Rollin oats, almond flour, raisins, sugar replacement, eggs, cinnamon, and vanilla essence should all be combined in a big basin.
3. Mix thoroughly to create a dough.
4. Drop dough onto ungreased baking sheets in a rounded spoonful.

SERVING SUGGESTIONS

Enjoy these wholesome oatmeal raisin cookies as a satisfying dessert or as a healthy snack. They are a pleasant treat for any occasion because of the combination of chewy oats, sweet raisins, and toasty spices.

PRESERVATION TIPS

To prolong the cookies' shelf life, freeze them or store them in an airtight container at room temperature.

EXTRA TIP(S)

Incorporate an additional ¼ cup of rolled oats into the dough for a chewy texture.

To give the dough a well-rounded flavor, add a small teaspoon of salt.

RECIPE 6: AVOCADO AND CHOCOLATE COOKIES

These delicious chocolate avocado cookies are a unique combination of rich cocoa and creamy avocado that will surprise you with their pleasure.

Estimated Yield: *18-24 cookies*
Preparation Time: *20-25 minutes*
Baking time: *10-12 minutes*

INGREDIENTS

1 cup of mashed avocado

½ cup chocolate powder, unsweetened

1 cup of almond flour

⅓ cup sugar alternative

A pinch of salt

½ teaspoon vanilla extract

METHOD OF PREPARATION

1. Set oven temperature to 175°C/350°F.

2. Mash the avocado until it's smooth and creamy in a big bowl.

3. Toss in the avocado with the unsweetened cocoa powder, almond flour, sugar substitute, vanilla extract, and salt.

4. Mix thoroughly to create a dough.

5. Dough tablespoons should be rolled into balls and then slightly flattened.

6. Place the cookies on a baking sheet that has not been oiled.

7. Bake for 10 to 12 minutes, or until the edges start to crisp up.

8. After taking the cookies out of the oven, allow them to cool for a few minutes on the baking sheet before moving them to a wire rack to finish cooling.

SERVING SUGGESTION

Enjoy the surprising fusion of chocolate and avocado in these rich cookies, which are ideal as a blameless treat or as a distinctive dessert choice.

PRESERVATION TIPS

To extend the cookies' shelf life, freeze them or keep them in an airtight container at room temperature.

EXTRA TIPS

Use dark, unsweetened cocoa powder for a deeper chocolate flavor. Before baking, top the cookies with chopped nuts for flavor and texture.

RECIPE 7: COOKIES WITH LEMON POPPY SEEDS

These cookies are full of vivid flavors from the poppy seeds and lemon zest, making them a delightful treat.

Estimated Yield: *18-22 cookies*
Preparation Time: *20-25 minutes*
Baking time: *10-12 minutes*

INGREDIENTS

1 cup of almond flour

2 teaspoons poppy seeds

1 lemon's zest

⅓ cup sugar alternative

1/2 cup of melted butter or coconut oil

1 teaspoon vanilla essence

METHOD OF PREPARATION

1. Set oven temperature to 175°C/350°F.
2. Almond flour, poppy seeds, lemon zest, sugar substitute, melted butter or coconut oil, and vanilla extract should all be combined in a big bowl and whisked until a dough forms.
3. Drop dough onto ungreased baking sheets in a rounded spoonful.
4. Bake for 10 to 12 minutes, until the edges start to turn a light golden brown.
5. After taking the cookies out of the oven, allow them to cool for a few minutes on the baking sheets before moving them to a wire rack to finish cooling.

SERVING SUGGESTIONS

These lemon poppy seed cookies are a delicious afternoon snack or great dessert alternative. Enjoy their zesty and refreshing flavors.

PRESERVATION TIPS

To prolong the cookies' shelf life, freeze them or store them in an airtight container at room temperature.

EXTRA TIP(S)

Add an extra teaspoon of lemon zest into the dough for a stronger lemon flavor.

For an added burst of sweetness, drizzle a straightforward sugar-free glaze over the cooled biscuits.

RECIPE 8: COOKIES WITH VANILLA AND ALMONDS

Accept the simplicity of these traditional, flavor-packed vanilla almond cookies, which are made with just a few ingredients.

Estimated Yield: *18-22 cookies*
Preparation Time: *15-20 minutes*
Baking time: *10-12* minutes

INGREDIENTS

¼ cup almond flour

⅓ cup sugar alternative

1/2 of melted butter or coconut oil

1 teaspoon vanilla essence

A dash of salt

METHOD OF PREPARATION

1. Set oven temperature to 175°C/350°F.
2. To make a dough, combine almond flour, sugar alternative, butter or coconut oil that has melted, vanilla extract, and salt in a big basin.
3. Drop dough onto ungreased baking sheets in a rounded spoonful.
4. Bake for 10 to 12 minutes, until the edges start to turn a light golden brown.
5. After taking the cookies out of the oven, allow them to cool for a few minutes on the baking sheets before moving them to a wire rack to finish cooling.

SERVING SUGGESTIONS

Enjoy the flavor of these vanilla almond cookies, which are easy to make and can be enjoyed blameless as a treat or as a daily snack.

PRESERVATION TIPS

To extend the cookies' shelf life, freeze them or keep them in an airtight container at room temperature.

EXTRA TIPS

Use toasted almond flour for a deeper taste.

A warm and inviting twist can be achieved by adding a pinch of nutmeg or cinnamon to the dough.

RECIPE 9: ORANGE-CRANBERRY COOKIES

Enjoy the bright, zesty tastes of these cranberry orange cookies—a delicious blend of sweet berries and festive citrus.

Estimated Yield: *20-24 cookies*

Preparation Time: *20-25 minutes*

Baking time: *10-12 minutes*

INGREDIENTS

¼ cup almond flour

½ cup of cranberries, dried

1 orange zest

⅓ cup sugar alternative

½ cup coconut oil or melted butter

1 teaspoon vanilla essence

METHOD OF PREPARATION

1. Turn the oven on to 325°F, or 165°C.

2. To make a dough, combine almond flour, sugar replacement, orange zest, melted butter or coconut oil, and vanilla essence in a large basin.

3. Drop dough onto ungreased baking sheets in a rounded spoonful.

4. Bake for 10 to 12 minutes, until the cranberries are starting to soften and the rims are golden brown.

5. After taking the cookies out of the oven, allow them to cool for a few minutes on the baking sheets before moving them to a wire rack to finish cooling.

SERVING SUGGESTION

Enjoy the fragrant and festive blend of orange and cranberries in these delicious cookies, ideal for a blameless treat or a Christmas get-together.

PRESERVATION TIPS

To extend the cookies' shelf life, freeze them or keep them in an airtight container at room temperature.

EXTRA TIP(S)

Incorporate an additional teaspoon of orange zest into the dough for a stronger orange taste.

For a rich treat, dip the cooled cookies into melted chocolate.

RECIPE 10: PEANUT BUTTER AND CHOCOLATE CHIPS COOKIES

These blameless peanut butter chocolate chip cookies are a delicious treat for any occasion. Enjoy the timeless pairing of peanut butter and chocolate.

Estimated Yield: *16-20 cookies*
Preparation Time: *15-20 minutes*
Baking time: *10-12 minutes*

INGREDIENTS

½ cup peanut butter and 1 cup almond flour

⅓ cup sugar alternative

½ teaspoon of baking powder

A dash of salt

½ cup chocolate chips without sugar

METHOD OF PREPARATION

1. Set oven temperature to 175°C/350°F.

2. Mix almond flour, peanut butter, sugar replacement, baking powder, and salt in a big basin until a dough forms.

3. Add the sugar-free chocolate chunks and fold gently.

4. Drop dough onto ungreased baking sheets in a rounded spoonful.

5. Bake for 10 to 12 minutes, until the centers are just beginning to soften and the sides are golden brown.

6. After taking the cookies out of the oven, allow them to cool for a few minutes on the baking sheets before moving them to a wire rack to finish cooling.

SERVING SUGGESTIONS

Snacking, dessert, or a special treat for peanut butter enthusiasts, these blameless cookies are the ultimate blend of peanut butter and chocolate.

PRESERVATION TIPS

To extend the cookies' shelf life, freeze them or keep them in an airtight container at room temperature.

EXTRA TIP(S)

Use dark roast peanut butter for a deeper peanut butter flavor. For a cozy and inviting addition, mix in a small amount of cinnamon into the dough.

RECIPE 11: CARDAMOM-WALNUT COOKIES

Enjoy the warm spice of cardamom in these delicious walnut cardamom cookies, which have a nutty and aromatic flavor.

Estimated Yield: *18-22 cookies*
Preparation Time: *15-20 minutes*
Baking time: *10-12 minutes*

INGREDIENTS

½ cup chopped walnuts

1 ½ cups almond flour

1 teaspoon of cardamom powder

⅓ cup sugar alternative

½ cup coconut oil or melted butter

1 teaspoon vanilla essence

METHOD OF PREPARATION

1. Turn the oven on to 325°F, or 165°C.

2. Combine almond flour, chopped walnuts, ground cardamom, sugar replacement, melted coconut oil or butter, and vanilla essence in a large bowl and mix until a dough forms.

3. Drop dough onto ungreased baking sheets in a rounded spoonful.

4. Bake for 10 to 12 minutes, or until the centers are just set and the rims are golden brown.

5. After taking the cookies out of the oven, allow them to cool for a few minutes on the baking sheets prior to moving them to a wire rack for final cooling.

SERVING SUGGESTION

Enjoy the delicious combination of cardamom and walnuts in these cookies, which are ideal for a blameless treat or a coffee break.

PRESERVATION TIPS

To extend the cookies' shelf life, freeze them or keep them in an airtight container at room temperature.

EXTRA TIP(S)

You can increase the amount of cardamom flavor in the dough by adding an extra ¼ teaspoon of ground cardamom.

For an additional layer of warmth, sprinkle the cooled cookies with a touch of nutmeg or cinnamon.

RECIPE 12: CHOCOLATE-MINT COOKIES

These blameless mint chocolate cookies are a tasty and fulfilling treat that let you satisfying the rich and refreshing taste of mint and chocolate.

Estimated Yield: 16-20 cookies
Preparation Time: 15-20 minutes
Baking time: 10-12 minutes

INGREDIENTS

½ cup unsweetened cocoa powder

1 ½ cups almond flour

⅓ cup sugar alternative

½ cup melted coconut oil

1 teaspoon of mint essence

1 teaspoon vanilla essence

METHOD OF PREPARATION

1. Set oven temperature to 175°C/350°F.

2. Almond flour, unsweetened cocoa powder, sugar substitute, melted coconut oil, mint extract, and vanilla extract should all be combined in a big basin and beaten until a dough forms.

3. Drop dough onto ungreased baking sheets in a rounded spoonful.

4. Bake for 10 to 12 minutes, until the centers are set and the sides are beginning to crisp.

5. After taking the cookies out of the oven, allow them to cool for a few minutes on the baking sheets before moving them to a wire rack to finish cooling.

SERVING SUGGESTIONS

enjoy the rich and cooling blend of chocolate and mint in these blameless cookies, which make a great afternoon snack or alternative dessert.

PRESERVATION TIPS

To extend the cookies' shelf life, freeze them or keep them in an airtight container at room temperature.

EXTRA TIP(S)

In order to achieve a stronger mint taste, incorporate an additional ¼ teaspoon of mint essence into the dough.

For a rich treat, dip the cooled cookies into melted chocolate

RECIPE 13: THUMBPRINT COOKIES WITH CHIA SEED JAM

These nutty almond flour thumbprint cookies with a sweet and tart chia seed jam filling will provide you with a pleasant flavor explosion.

Estimated Yield: *18-22 cookies*
Preparation time: *20-25 minutes*
Baking time: *10-12 minutes*

INGREDIENTS

¼ cup almond flour

⅓ cup sugar alternative

½ cup melted coconut oil

1 teaspoon vanilla essence

A dash of salt

For The Chia Seed Jam

¼ cup of chia seeds

¼ cup sugar substitute

½ cup of water

¼ cup mashed fresh or frozen berries

METHOD OF PREPARATION

1. Set oven temperature to 350°F (175°C)

2. Almond flour, sugar substitute, melted coconut oil, vanilla extract, and salt should all be combined in a big basin and beaten into a dough

3. Drop a spoonful of dough onto ungreased baking pans and roll into balls.

4. Make an indentation in the middle of each cookie with your thumb.

To Make The Chia Seed Jam:

A) Put the chia seeds, sugar substitute, and water in a small pot.

B) After bringing to a simmer, lower the heat, and simmer the mixture for five minutes, or until it thickens.

C) Take off the heat and mix in the mashed blueberries

- Spoon the chia seed jam into the cookie indentations.
- Bake the cookies for 10 to 12 minutes, or until the edges turn golden brown.
- After taking the cookies out of the oven, allow them to cool for a few minutes on the baking sheets before moving them to a wire rack to finish cooling.

SERVING

Enjoy the delicious combination of sweet and tart chia seed jam and nutty almond flour cookies in these thumbprint cookies makes them ideal for a blameless treat or a novel dessert alternative.

PRESERVATION TIPS

The cookies can be kept for up to three days at room temperature in an airtight container.

EXTRA TIP(S)

Try combining several berry varieties, including raspberries, blueberries, and strawberries, for a stronger berry flavor.

Before you fill the cookies, sprinkle a little cinnamon over the chia seed jam to provide a little extra warmth.

RECIPE 14: COOKIES WITH HAZELNUT ESPRESSO

Enjoy the flavorful and complex aromas of these hazelnut espresso cookies, an ideal dessert for coffee connoisseurs and anybody looking for a luxurious treat.

Estimated Yield: *20-24 cookies*
Preparation Time: *20-25 minutes*
Baking time: *10-12 minutes*

INGREDIENTS

1 ½ cups almond flour

½ cup finely crushed hazelnuts

1 scoop of instant espresso powder

⅓ cup sugar substitute

½ cup melted butter or coconut oil

1 teaspoon of pure vanilla

¼ cup sugar-free dark chocolate chunks or chips (optional)

METHOD OF PREPARATION

1. Preheat the oven to 175°C/350°F.

2. In a big basin, mix almond flour, sugar substitute, ground hazelnuts, melted butter or coconut oil, and vanilla essence to form a dough.

3. If using, gently incorporate the chocolate chunks into the dough.

4. By spoonfuls, drop dough onto ungreased baking sheets.

5. Bake for 10 to 12 minutes, until the centers are just beginning to soften and the sides are golden brown.

6. After taking the cookies out of the oven, allow them to cool for a few minutes on the baking sheets before moving them to a wire rack to finish cooling.

SERVING SUGGESTION

Enjoy these flavorful and creamy hazelnut espresso cookies as a sumptuous dessert or as a treat in the afternoon. They're a lovely treat for any occasion, with their powerful espresso flavor, nutty hazelnuts, and subtle sweetness.

PRESERVATION TIPS

To extend the cookies' shelf life, freeze them or keep them in an airtight container at room temperature for up to three days.

EXTRA TIP(S)

In order to achieve a stronger espresso taste, add an additional ¼ teaspoon of instant espresso powder into the dough.

For a contrast of sweetness and salt, sprinkle a small amount of sea salt on top of the cookies prior to baking.

RECIPE 15: COOKIES WITH SALTED CARAMEL FILLING

Enjoy the combination of sweet and salty taste with these shortbread biscuits and salted caramel which are a rich and filling treat.

Estimated Yield: *18-22 cookies*

Preparation Time: *20-25 minutes*

Baking time: *10-12 minutes*

INGREDIENTS

1 ½ cups almond flour

½ cup coconut oil or melted butter

⅓ cup sugar alternative

A dash of salt

For The Caramel With Salt:

¼ cup sugar substitute

½ cup thick cream

¼ cup of finely chopped butter

A dash of salt

METHOD OF PREPARATION

1. Set oven temperature to 350°F (175°C).

2. Mix the almond flour, coconut oil or melted butter, sugar replacement, and salt in a big basin until a dough forms.

3. Grease an 8 × 8-inch baking pan and evenly press the dough into it.

4. Bake dough for 15 to 20 minutes until the edges are golden brown.

5. As the shortbread bakes, get the salted caramel ready.

Salted Caramel Preparation

- In a saucepan, melt the sugar substitute over a medium heat.

- After the sugar substitute melts, mix in the heavy cream bit by bit.

- Whisk the mixture until it thickens and reaches a simmer.

- Take off the heat and slowly whisk in the butter, little by bit, until it becomes creamy.

- Add the salt and stir.

A) Evenly sprinkle the salted caramel over the baked shortbread after pouring it over.

B) Top with a small pinch of sea salt.

C) Put the caramel in the refrigerator for at least half an hour, or until it sets.

D) Square them up and eat.

SERVING SUGGESTION

Enjoy the rich and luscious blend of sweet and salty in these shortbread cookies with salted caramel; they're ideal as a blameless dinner or as a treat in the afternoon. Your taste buds will be tempted by the delectable delight created by the contrast between the creamy salted caramel and the buttery shortbread.

PRESERVATION TIPS

To extend the cookies' shelf life, freeze them or keep them in an airtight container at room temperature for up to three days.

EXTRA TIP(S)

Use dark roast almond flour for a deeper caramel flavor.

A hint of cinnamon added to the shortbread crust will give it a cozy and welcoming twist.

RECIPE 16: SNICKERDOODLES WITH PUMPKIN SPICE

These soft and chewy pumpkin spice snickerdoodles are a great way to embrace the flavors of fall. They are flavored with the warm spices of pumpkin pie.

Estimated Yield: *16-20 cookies*
Preparation Time: *20-25 minutes*
Baking Time: *10-12 minutes*

INGREDIENTS

½ cup almond flour

½ cup pureed pumpkin

⅓ cup sugar alternative

¼ cup coconut oil or melted butter

1 teaspoon pumpkin spice mixture

A dash of salt

About the non-Sugar Coating of Cinnamon:

⅓ cup sugar alternative

2 teaspoon finely ground cinnamon

METHOD OF PREPARATION

1. Set oven temperature to 175°C/350°F.

2. To make a dough, combine almond flour, sugar alternative, melted butter or coconut oil, pumpkin puree, pumpkin spice blend, and salt in a big basin.

3. Ground cinnamon and sugar substitute should be combined in a shallow basin.

4. Coat each dough ball evenly with the cinnamon sugar coating by rolling it in it.

5. Transfer covered dough balls to baking sheets that have not been greased.

6. Bake for 10 to 12 minutes, or until the centers are set and the rims are golden brown.

7. After taking the cookies out of the oven, allow them to cool for a few minutes on the baking sheets before moving them to a wire rack to finish cooling.

SERVING SUGGESTIONS

These pumpkin spice snickerdoodles are a great afternoon snack or blameless dessert choice. They bring cozy, fall flavors to your palate.

The flavors of pumpkin pie infuse the soft and chewy cookies to produce a wonderful dessert that will provide a cozy, comforting touch to any event.

PRESERVATION TIPS

To extend the cookies' shelf life, freeze them or keep them in an airtight container at room temperature for up to three days.

EXTRA TIP(S)

Use homemade pumpkin puree for a stronger pumpkin taste.

To give the dough an additional layer of warmth, mix in a pinch of nutmeg.

RECIPE 17: ALMOND COOKIES WITH DARK CHOCOLATE

Without sacrificing your health, these rich dark chocolate almond cookies are the ideal way to satisfy your sweet craving. These cookies are a rich and filling treat that are made with almond flour, unsweetened cocoa powder, sugar substitute, melted coconut oil, almond extract, and sugar-free dark chocolate chunks or chips.

Estimated Yield: *20-24 cookies*
Preparation Time: *20-25 minutes*
Baking time : *10-12 minutes*

INGREDIENTS

½ cup almond flour

½ cup of unsweetened cocoa powder

⅓ cup sugar alternative

¼ cup melted coconut oil

½ teaspoon of almond extract

Dark chocolate chips or chunks without added sugar.

METHOD OF PREPARATION

1. Set oven temperature to 175°C/350°F.

2. Mix almond flour, cocoa powder, sugar replacement, and almond extract in a big bowl until a dough forms.

3. Stir in the melted coconut oil until a dough forms.

4. Stir in chips or chunks of sugar-free dark chocolate.

5. Drop dough onto ungreased baking sheets in a rounded spoonful.

6. Bake for 10 to 12 minutes, or until cookies are firm and have a hint of golden color around the edges.

7. After a few minutes, let the cookies cool on the baking sheets before moving them to a wire rack to cool fully.

SERVING

Enjoy these rich almond biscuits with dark chocolate guilt-free.

PRESERVATION TIPS

Freeze for extended storage or keep in an airtight container at room temperature.

EXTRA TIP(S)

Use dark roast almond flour for a deeper taste.

For a contrast of sweet and salt, mix in a small teaspoon of sea salt into the dough.

RECIPE 18: PISTACHIO CARDAMOM BISCOTTI

Dip these crispy biscotti into coffee or tea for the ultimate indulgence. Almond flour, melted butter or coconut oil, ground cardamom, chopped pistachios, and vanilla extract are the ingredients.

Estimated Yield: *16-20 biscotti*
Preparation Time*: 20-25 minutes*
Baking Time: *25-30 minutes (first bake), 10-12 minutes (second bake)*

INGREDIENTS

½ cup chopped pistachios

2 cups almond flour

1 teaspoon of cardamom powder

⅓ cup sugar alternative

¼ cup coconut oil or melted butter

½ teaspoon of vanilla extract

METHOD OF PREPARATION

1. Turn the oven on to 325°F, or 165°C.

2. Almond flour, pistachios, powder cardamom, sugar replacement, melted butter or coconut oil, and vanilla essence should all be combined in a big basin and whisked until a dough forms.

3. Form the dough into two logs each about 10 inches long and 2 inches wide.

4. Bake these logs for 25 to 30 minutes, or until golden brown, on an oiled baking sheet.

5. Take it out of the oven and let it cool down a little.

6. Cut the logs into ½-inch-thick slices using a diagonal cut.

7. Reposition the biscotti slices on the baking sheet, and bake for 10 to 12 minutes, or just until they are beginning to brown.

8. Before storing, allow the biscotti to cool fully on a wire rack.

SERVING SUGGESTION

Enjoy these crispy biscotti with a cup of tea or coffee without any sugar.

PRESERVATION TIPS

To extend the shelf life, freeze or store in an airtight container.

EXTRA TIP(S)

Use salted and roasted pistachios for a stronger taste of pistachios.

For a cozy and inviting addition, mix in a small amount of cinnamon into the dough.

RECIPE 19: COOKIES WITH MAPLE AND PECANS

Enjoy the lovely aromas of maple and pecans with these chewy, soft maple pecan cookies. Ingredients: almond flour, chopped pecans, melted coconut oil or butter, sugar substitute, chopped nuts, and vanilla essence.

Estimated Yield: *18-22 cookies*
Preparation Time: *20-25 minutes*
Baking Time: *12-15 minutes*

INGREDIENTS

1½ cups of almond flour

½ cup of pecans, chopped

¼ cup maple syrup without sugar

⅓ cup sugar alternative

¼ cup coconut oil or melted butter

½ teaspoon of vanilla extract.

METHOD OF PREPARATION

1. Set oven temperature to 175°C/350°F.

2. To make a dough, combine almond flour, chopped nuts, sugar-free maple syrup, melted coconut oil or butter, and vanilla essence in a large bowl.

3. Drop dough onto ungreased baking sheets in a rounded spoonful.

4. Bake for a total of 12 to 15 minutes, or until the edges are golden brown and firm.

5. After taking the cookies out of the oven, allow them to cool for a few minutes on the baking sheets before moving them to a wire rack to finish cooling.

SERVING SUGGESTIONS

Enjoy the delicious combination of nuts and maple in these chewy, soft cookies, which are ideal as a blameless treat or as a midday snack. They are a delicious treat that anybody can enjoy, thanks to the nutty crunch of the nuts and the warm, inviting flavor of maple syrup.

PRESERVATION TIPS

To extend the cookies' shelf life, freeze them or keep them in an airtight container at room temperature for up to three days.

EXTRA TIP(S)

You can increase the amount of maple flavor in the dough by adding an extra tablespoon of sugar-free maple syrup.

For a contrast of sweetness and salt, sprinkle a small amount of sea salt on top of the cookies prior to baking.

RECIPE 20: ALMOND COOKIES WITH DOUBLE CHOCOLATE

These delicious double chocolate almond cookies are created with almond flour, sugar alternative, unsweetened cocoa powder, melted butter or coconut oil, almond extract, and sugar-free chocolate chunks or chips. Enjoy the ultimate chocolate experience with these.

Estimated Yield: *20-24 cookies*
Preparation Time: *20-25 minutes*
Baking time : *10-12 minutes*

INGREDIENTS

½ Cup almond flour

½ Cup of unsweetened cocoa powder

⅓ cup sugar alternative

¼ cup coconut oil or melted butter

½ teaspoon of almond extract

½ cup sugar-free chips or chunks of dark chocolate

METHOD OF PREPARATION

1. Set oven temperature to 175°C/350°F.
2. Mix the almond flour, cocoa powder, sugar substitute, melted coconut oil or butter, and almond extract in a big basin until a dough forms.
3. Stir in chips or chunks of sugar-free dark chocolate until well distributed.
4. Drop dough onto ungreased baking sheets in a rounded spoonful.
5. Bake for 10 to 12 minutes, until the centers are set and the sides are beginning to crisp.
6. After taking the cookies out of the oven, allow them to cool for a few minutes on the baking sheets before moving them to a wire rack to finish cooling.

SERVING SUGGESTION

These double chocolate almond cookies are ideal for any chocolate enthusiast because of their rich and luscious flavors. They are incredibly delicious due to the rich chocolate taste and the nutty deliciousness of almond flour.

PRESERVATION TIPS

To extend the cookies' shelf life, freeze them or keep them in an airtight container at room temperature for up to three days.

EXTRA TIP(S)

Use dark roast almond flour and dark unsweetened cocoa powder for a deeper chocolate flavor.

For a contrast of sweetness and salt, sprinkle a small amount of sea salt on top of the cookies prior to baking.

BONUS CHAPTER: FESTIVE PACKAGING IDEAS

Here are some creative and festive packaging ideas that can be used to present these sugar-free cookies to your family and friends

1. DECORATIVE COOKIE TINS

- Choose tins with festive designs such as snowflakes, Santa Claus, candy canes, or holiday landscapes that have airtight seals to maintain cookie freshness.
- Select tins of appropriate sizes based on the quantity of cookies to be gifted. Offer various sizes to accommodate small batches or larger assortments.
- Ensure the tins are clean and dry before placing the cookies iinside.

- Line the bottom of the tin with parchment paper or food-safe tissue paper for added protection.
- Arrange the cookies neatly inside the tin, leaving enough space between each cookie to prevent breakage or sticking together during transportation.
- wrap a festive ribbon around the tin or attach a bow for an extra decorative touch.
- Close the tin securely to preserve the cookies' freshness. Ensure the lid is properly sealed and secure it with tape or additional wrapping if necessary.
- Complement the ribbon color with the tin's design.
- Present the decorated cookie tin as a standalone gift or add it into a larger gift basket or collection of holiday treats.
- Personalize the tins by adding the recipient's name or a special message using stickers, labels, or custom, a holiday message, or a brief description of the cookies inside with preservation for a thoughtful touch.

2. DIY COOKIE GIFT BASKETS

- Use decorative wicker baskets, trays, or boxes as the base for the DIY gift baskets. Ensure the size accommodates the cookies and additional items

- Line the bottom of the baskets with a festive cloth, paper napkins, or shredded paper for a decorative foundation.

- Arrange cookies in an aesthetically pleasing manner inside the basket. Consider using cupcake liners or tissue paper for separation

- Include complementary items such as a small jar of sugar-free jam, a decorative kitchen towel, or a handwritten recipe card to enhance the gift basket.

- Add a ribbon bow to the basket's handle or tie a ribbon around the entire basket for a polished and festive look.

- Attach a personalized gift tag or card to the basket conveying warm wishes or a personalized message for the recipient.

3. HOLIDAY-THEMED TISSUE PAPER

- Use a suitable holiday-themed tissue paper as a cushioning layer inside gift boxes, bags, or baskets.
- Crinkle or fold the tissue paper neatly for an attractive presentation.
- Store unused tissue paper in a clean, dry place to prevent creasing or damage and encourage recipients to reuse the tissue paper for future gift packaging.
- Personalize the tissue paper by adding hand-drawn designs, stamps, or stickers that reflect the holiday theme. Consider using custom-printed tissue paper for a branded touch.

4. CLEAR CELLOPHANE BAGS WITH DECORATIVE ACCENTS

- Choose food-safe, clear cellophane bags in various sizes suitable for packaging cookies.
- Ensure the bags are durable and transparent to showcase the cookies.
- Arrange cookies inside the bags, ensuring they are placed neatly and uniformly. Consider grouping similar cookies or creating a variety pack.
- Gather the bag's opening and secure it with a festive twist tie, a decorative ribbon, or colorful washi tape to seal and embellish the package.
- Add additional decorative elements like seasonal stickers, small ornaments, or personalized gift tags tied onto the bag's closure for a festive touch.

5. PERSONALIZED COOKIE SLEEVES OR WRAPPERS

- create personalized sleeves or wrappers using decorative paper, cardstock, or printable templates. Ensure the material is food-safe and easy to fold or wrap around the cookies.
- Add personalized messages, recipients' names, or holiday-themed designs to the sleeves.
- Assemble the sleeves around the cookies securely
- Use double-sided tape, glue dots, or adhesive stickers to seal the edges of the wrappers or sleeves. Ensure the closure is secure yet easy to open.

6. HOLIDAY-THEMED TISSUE PAPER

- choose suitable holiday-themed tissue paper in vibrant colors or patterns. Use red, green, or metallic shades to enhance the festive appeal.

- Use the tissue paper for layering between cookies or as a cushioning layer inside gift boxes or bags. This protects the cookies while adding visual interest.
- Fold the tissue paper neatly or crinkle it to create texture.use it as a base or backdrop when displaying cookies for a decorative effect.
- Mix and match different tissue paper colors or patterns to create visually appealing combinations, adding depth to the presentation.

7. DECORATIVE PLATTERS

- Choose platters that match the holiday theme or reflect an elegant presentation.
- Opt for materials like ceramic, glass, or decorative trays that suit the occasion.

- Place the sugar-free cookies on the platter, layering them with care to create an appealing arrangement. Consider placing larger cookies at the base and smaller ones on top for variety.

- To prevent direct contact with the platter, use festive cupcake liners or food-safe parchment paper beneath the cookies. This adds a decorative touch and safeguards the platter.

- Create visual interest by mixing different shapes, sizes, and colors of cookies on the platter. Group similar cookies or alternate between various types for an attractive display.

- If presenting cookies on multiple platters, consider arranging them at varying heights using tiered stands. Add decorative elements like ribbons or greenery for a festive touch.

8. STACKED COOKIE TUBES:

- Choose clear or decorated tubes with secure lids that fit the cookies snugly. Opt for transparent tubes to showcase the cookies and select lids that seal tightly.
- Stack cookies inside the tubes in layers, separating each layer with twist-off lids or parchment paper circles. This prevents cookies from sticking and maintains their shape.
- Ensure each cookie layer is secured with the tube's lid to prevent shifting or breakage during transportation.
- Add tissue paper or bubble wrap between layers for added protection.
- Offer a variety of cookie types in each tube or stack tubes of different cookie varieties for an assorted gift. Mix contrasting colors or shapes for an eye-catching display.
- Tie festive ribbons around each tube or stack, creating a visually appealing presentation.

- Consider arranging tubes in a gift basket or adding tags for personalization.

9. THEMED COOKIE TOTES:

- Choose themed tote bags made of durable material that complements the holiday theme. Opt for bags with ample space to accommodate the cookies comfortably.
- Line the bottom of the tote bags with themed tissue paper or cloth for a decorative base.
- Arrange the sugar-free cookies inside, ensuring they're secured and well-positioned.
- To protect the cookies during transportation, consider using small boxes or food-safe bags within the tote bags to keep cookies separated and intact.
- Offer a variety of cookie types or shapes within the tote bags to create a diverse assortment.

- Mix different flavors or sizes for a delightful gift presentation.

- Tie the tote bag handles with vibrant ribbons or attach personalized tags to enhance the presentation.

- Present the tote bags individually or as part of a larger gift arrangement.

10. MASON JARS WITH RIBBON TIES

- Choose clean and dry mason jars with alrtight lids to preserve cookie freshness. Offer different jar sizes based on the number of cookies to be gifted.

- Stack or arrange cookies neatly inside the jars. Use parchment paper or cupcake liners between layers to prevent sticking.

- Tie a colorful ribbon or twine around the jar's neck. Add a small ornament, jingle bell, or a sprig of holly to the ribbon for a festive touch.

- Create custom labels or tags for the jars. Include details such as the cookie type, a heartfelt message, or baking instructions if applicable.

- Presenting the decorated mason jars individually or as part of a larger gift collection. They can also be arranged in a basket or tray for a charming display.

CONCLUSION

As we arrive at the final page of DIABETIC -FRIENDLY CHRISTMAS COOKIES RECIPES COOKBOOK , I'm filled with immense gratitude for the opportunity to share these culinary delights with you.

This cookbook is more than just a collection of recipes; it's a celebration of flavors, traditions, and the joy of creating delicious meals.

To each reader who has journeyed through these recipes, I extend my heartfelt thanks. Your willingness to explore these culinary paths, try new flavors, and adopt the art of cooking has made this journey truly special. As you continue to savor these recipes and craft tasty bites, may the aromas, tastes, and shared moments linger as cherished memories in your kitchen and at your table. May these dishes bring comfort, joy, and a sense of togetherness to your gatherings.

Lastly, with the holiday season upon us, I wish you and your loved ones a festive and delightful celebration. May your kitchen be filled with laughter, warmth, and the delightful aromas of delicious cookies. Thank you for allowing these recipes to become a part of your culinary repertoire. Your support and enthusiasm have made this cookbook a flavorful exploration. Wishing you a season filled with culinary delights and heartwarming moments around the table, *thank you!*.

Merry Christmas and a Happy New Year!!!